CACTUS

CAROL LERNER

MORROW JUNIOR BOOKS

NEW YORK

For my editor, Andrea Curley, who had the good idea

Acknowledgments

Illustrations of Euphorbia flowers on page 9 are based on *The Succulent Euphor-bieae* by Alain White, R. Allen Dyer, and Boyd L. Sloan (Pasadena, Ca.: Abbey Garden Press, 1941), vol. 2, plate 22. The illustration on page 22 (*left*) is based on *The Illustrated Encyclopedia of Cacti and Other Succulents* by J. Říha and R. Šubík (London: Octopus Books, 1981), page 13.

The author thanks Dr. Arthur C. Gibson of the Department of Biology, University of California at Los Angeles, for his comments on the manuscript.

Watercolors were used for the full-color artwork. The text type is 15 point Horley Old Style.

Printed in Singapore at Tien Wah Press.

1   2   3   4   5   6   7   8   9   10

Library of Congress Cataloging-in-Publication Data
Lerner, Carol.
Cactus / by Carol Lerner.
p.   cm.
Summary: Discusses the physical characteristics, growth patterns, habitats, and varieties of cacti.
ISBN 0-688-09636-0 (trade) —ISBN 0-688-09637-9 (library)
1. Cactus—Juvenile literature. [1. Cactus.] I. Title.
QK495.C11L43 1992
583′.47—dc20   91-35678 CIP AC

CONTENTS

ONE

THE CACTUS STEM

You probably think that you know a cactus when you see one. Whether it is small or large, squat or tall, the typical cactus has a thick, chunky shape that sets it apart from other plants.

What you are seeing is actually just a cactus *stem*. Like an elm tree in winter, standing without its summer leaves, a cactus plant is a bare stem. But unlike the trunk and branches of the tree, the stem of the cactus is green and is not wrapped in a layer of bark. Nor does the cactus depend on leaves to make its food, as the tree does. It can live through all the seasons of the year without them.

Botanists think that the earliest cacti had ordinary, flat leaves growing from ordinary plant stems. At that distant time, cacti probably looked much like other kinds of plants. The green chlorophyll that is necessary to turn raw materials into food was in the cactus leaves, as it is in most plants.

Over the centuries, as the seeds of these early cacti were spread, some of the plants began to grow in places with drier climates. And gradually the cacti in those dry habitats began to change. Like all desert plants, they had to have some way of staying alive during long rainless periods. Part of the solution was the development of thick stems that could store water for use in time of drought.

The greatest part of a cactus stem is made up of special water storage cells. The wall around each of these large cells is thin and elastic. Whenever there is rain, the cactus absorbs it quickly and the storage cells fill with water. After a good rainfall, the plant consists mostly of water—90 percent or more. In dry weather, the cactus draws upon this supply.

The earliest cacti probably changed very slowly. Gradually, as one generation of plants followed the last, their stems became thicker. And as the stems grew in size and importance, there were other changes. Chlorophyll appeared in the enlarged stems, and finally the stems took over the work of making the plants' food.

Now leaves were a disadvantage. No longer needed for food manufacture, they shaded the plant and kept the sun's rays from reaching the chlorophyll in the stem. Slowly, leaves on desert cacti began to disappear, becoming smaller and smaller over the generations.

With a thick, leafless stem, a plant's fitness for life in dry climates improves enormously. A plant loses water into the air from every square inch of its surface—from the stem, leaves, flowers, and fruits. If the plant has many large leaves, the moisture loss can be tremendous. A medium-sized elm tree, for example, may give off a ton of water in a single summer day!

Plants growing where there is little rainfall have no way of replacing such a huge water loss, but they can survive by conserving the small amounts of water they do receive. One way to conserve moisture is to expose less surface area to the drying air. With smaller leaves, fewer leaves, or none at all, a plant's water loss is much less.

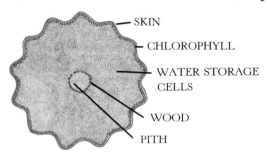

SKIN

CHLOROPHYLL

WATER STORAGE CELLS

WOOD

PITH

If you sliced through a cactus stem, you would see that most of it is used for storage. Just under the skin there is a thin green layer of cells containing the microscopic bits of chlorophyll. Next to it is a large colorless area filled with the water storage cells. The pulp here is like the flesh of a watery melon.

Almost all cacti have some woody tissue near the center of the stem. The cylinder of wood is thin except in the larger cactus species. This wood skeleton helps support the weight of a water-laden cactus. At the very center of the stem is the pith, containing still more water-storage cells.

Most cactus stems do not have flat surfaces. Many are covered by small humps that make a series of little hills and valleys over the outside of the stem. On other cacti, the humps are arranged in a line, forming a series of ribs that run up and down the stem. The uneven surface makes it possible for the stems to expand without splitting their skins.

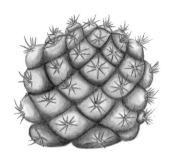

Surfaces of cactus stems

If you look at the cross section of a ribbed cactus before and after a rainfall, you can see how this works. The stem folds and opens like an accordion. After a dry period, the stem shrinks and there are deep grooves between each rib. When it rains, the ribs swell as the stem absorbs water and the grooves become flatter.

Cross section of a ribbed cactus stem before rainfall (top) and after

All plants that can hoard large amounts of water are called *succulents*. The succulent part of a plant—the part that stores the water—may be its leaves, its underground parts, or (as in a cactus) its stem. The succulent part is usually thick and juicy.

Succulence is an effective way of getting through long dry seasons. About ten thousand species of plants, scattered among thirty-three different plant families, have some degree of succulence in their leaves, roots, or stems.

Like succulence, having thick, green, leafless stems is not unique to the cactus family. Cacti are native plants only in the Americas, but many plants from other parts of the world look like their twins. In response to similar desert conditions, they too have developed cactus-like forms. Some of the most striking look-alikes are found in Africa. These are Euphorbia (you-FOR-bee-uh) plants belonging to the spurge family. They have thick, green stems. Some have thorns. And at first glance, they look just like a cactus.

But botanists concentrate on a plant's flowers and fruits to understand plant relationships, and these cactus-like spurge plants have flower structures that are completely different from those of the cacti. Spurge flowers are small and inconspicuous, without large bright petals. They grow together in groups, inside a tiny cup-like structure. Most people would have trouble even recognizing them as flowers.

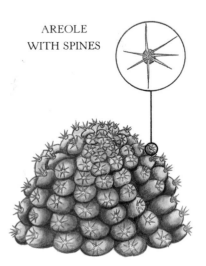

AREOLE
WITH SPINES

Even without the evidence of a flower or fruit, it is possible to distinguish a cactus from one of its foreign twins, if you look closely. All members of the cactus family carry a telltale mark on the skin of their stems—a series of little bumps called *areoles* ("little areas"). These have not been found in any other plant family.

Areoles are covered by a little pad of hair. Other kinds of plant growth may spring from the areoles, too: cactus spines, side branches of the stem, flowers and fruits, and even—in a few species—full-sized leaves!

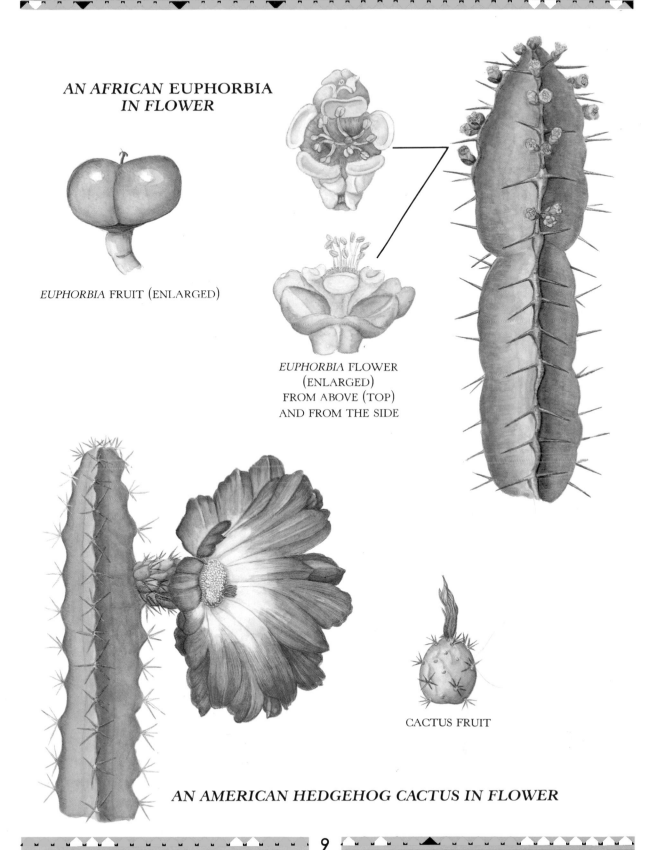

AN AFRICAN EUPHORBIA IN FLOWER

EUPHORBIA FRUIT (ENLARGED)

EUPHORBIA FLOWER
(ENLARGED)
FROM ABOVE (TOP)
AND FROM THE SIDE

CACTUS FRUIT

AN AMERICAN HEDGEHOG CACTUS IN FLOWER

THE CACTUS FAMILY

Fossils showing imprints of ancient living forms sometimes give hints about the development of plant and animal life on earth. Botanists struggling to understand the history of the cactus family have had to work without these clues, for there is no fossil record of the cactus past. The evidence must come from looking at living species.

There is no shortage of these, for it is a large family. There may be more than fifteen hundred different species of cacti, but the botanists are not in agreement on this. Some put the number of species at well over two thousand.

One branch of botany is devoted to sorting the species into groups that share important characteristics. The plant *family* is one such group. Botanists sometimes divide the plants in a family into smaller groups called *subfamilies*. The cactus family is divided into three subfamilies.

The plants within each subfamily that appear to be very close relatives of one another are put into a still-smaller group called a *genus*. (The plural of *genus* is *genera*.) And finally, the members of a genus are separated into different *species*. Plants of the same species are judged to be alike in all important respects.

Just as there is no agreement about the number of different cactus species, there is none on the number of cactus genera. Different authorities have put the total as low as thirty or as high as two hundred

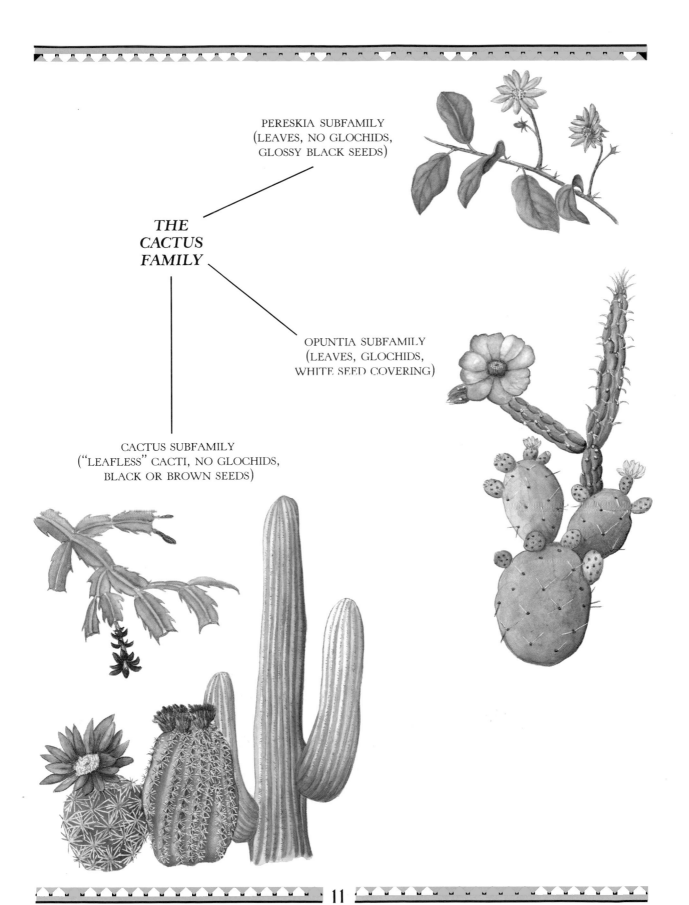

PERESKIA SUBFAMILY
(LEAVES, NO GLOCHIDS,
GLOSSY BLACK SEEDS)

THE
CACTUS
FAMILY

OPUNTIA SUBFAMILY
(LEAVES, GLOCHIDS,
WHITE SEED COVERING)

CACTUS SUBFAMILY
("LEAFLESS" CACTI, NO GLOCHIDS,
BLACK OR BROWN SEEDS)

and twenty. The botanists do agree that one small genus of cactus plants containing sixteen species probably resembles the ancestors of a typical modern cactus. This genus is called *Pereskia* (puh-RESK-ee-uh). It was named to honor Nicolas-Claude Fabri de Peiresc, a French scholar and naturalist of the early seventeenth century who had broad interests in the sciences. (The *i* in his name was lost along the way.)

Although you probably think of them as desert plants, not all cacti live in dry places. *Pereskia* plants are natives of the American tropics from Mexico to Argentina, as well as the West Indies. They grow as bushes, vines, or trees, living in habitats where they do not have to cope with extreme dryness.

Pereskia plants look nothing like the typical cactus plant, for they have large green leaves growing along their branches. But their proof of membership in the cactus family is found in the small round areole located at the point where each leaf is attached to the stem. The areole also bears one or more spines.

Pereskia flowers grow near the tips of their branches. Flowers of most species in the genus show an arrangement of parts that is found in almost all cacti.

A typical flower has four main parts. Going from the outer ring to the center, they are: the sepals, which wrap the flower bud before it opens; the petals; the pollen-bearing male stamens; and the female pistil. In a typical flower, it is easy to see the difference between the green sepals and the bright petals. In most cactus flowers, however, this difference is not sharp, because the inner circles of sepals gradually become more and more petal-like. Botanists therefore use special words when describing cactus flowers. Instead of sepals and petals, they call these parts *sepaloids* and *petaloids*.

All cactus flowers have many stamens, as the *Pereskia* does. In some cactus species, the number is enormous: the blossom of the giant saguaro cactus, for instance, was found to have 3,400 stamens.

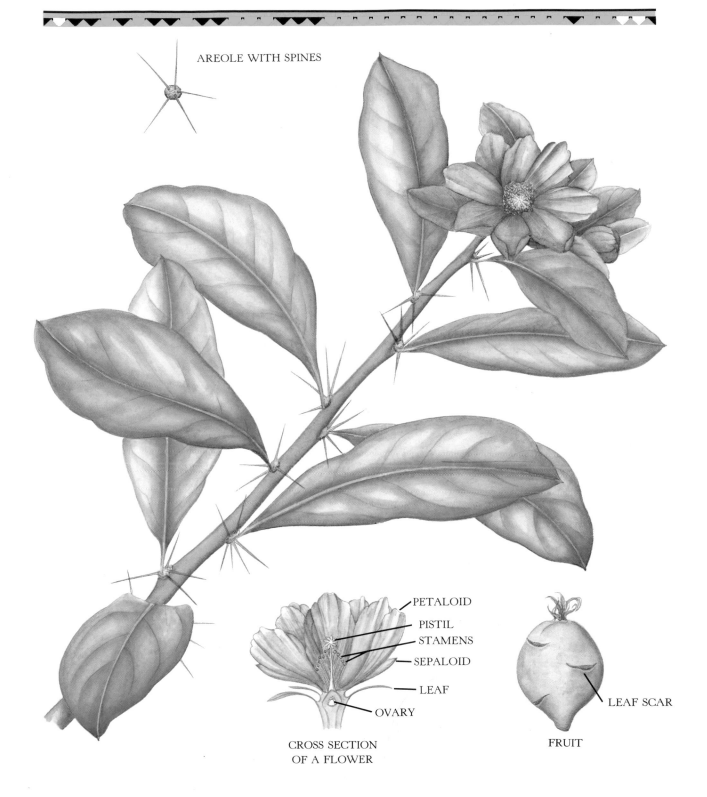

AREOLE WITH SPINES

PETALOID

PISTIL

STAMENS

SEPALOID

LEAF

OVARY

CROSS SECTION
OF A FLOWER

LEAF SCAR

FRUIT

A PERESKIA CACTUS

The pistil is at the center of the flower. The swollen part at the bottom of the pistil is the ovary, where a fruit containing the plant's seeds is formed. In the *Pereskia* flower shown here, as in almost all cactus species, the ovary is below the point where the sepals and petals appear to be attached to the flower. In botanical language, this is called an inferior ovary. (The original meaning of "inferior" is "below" or "underneath.")

The arrangement of the flower parts is even clearer when you look at the *Pereskia* fruit. Like all fruits, it grows from the fertilized ovary. You can see what is left of the petals, stamens, and pistil on the very top of the young *Pereskia* fruit.

Many kinds of plants have flowers with inferior ovaries. Cactus flowers are unusual because their ovaries have apparently sunk down into a portion of the cactus stem. The surrounding stem material becomes part of the cactus fruit that develops from the ovary. You can see that this *Pereskia* fruit is covered with stem tissue: it has scars on its outside surface showing where leaves were attached earlier. Other kinds of cacti have fruits that are covered with areoles and spines.

Pereskia plants are believed to show an early stage in the development of the cactus family. Botanists put them and one other very small genus, called *Maihuenia* (my-WHANE-ee-uh), into a separate subfamily within the larger cactus family. The subfamily is named after the *Pereskia* genus, since that is considered to be the more important of these two genera.

Still another small cactus genus with flat leaves has been given the name *Pereskiopsis* (puh-resk-ee-OP-sis), meaning "like the *Pereskia*." This genus, containing about ten species, grows in Mexico and Guatemala. In spite of the broad leaves that it shares with *Pereskia*, botanists put *Pereskiopsis* into a different subfamily, the Opuntia (oh-PUNCH-ee-uh) subfamily.

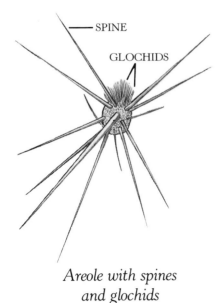

SPINE

GLOCHIDS

Areole with spines and glochids

Pereskiopsis areoles have a bristly growth that is never found on members of the Pereskia subfamily. These tiny bristles, called *glochids*, are in addition to the spines and the little pads of hair found on cactus areoles. Unlike spines, which stay firmly in place, glochids come off at the slightest touch. Even a strong wind can detach them. But once off the plant, they stick like glue. If you look at a glochid through a magnifying glass, you can see why this is so. Each one has dozens of tiny barbs along its entire length.

The seeds of *Pereskiopsis* cacti also set them apart. In contrast to the black, glossy seeds of the Pereskia subfamily, *Pereskiopsis* seeds have a special kind of white outer covering. This special covering is hard and bonelike.

Leaves, glochids, and this special seed covering are the signs of membership in the second subfamily. It is named after the most important genus it contains, the *Opuntia*. This is a very old name that was used by European botanists as far back as the sixteenth century. It is said to come from the name

The top part of a glochid (much enlarged)

of a town in Greece where some kind of prickly plants grew.

Opuntia is the largest and most widespread genus in the entire cactus family, with over one hundred and sixty species. Most *Opuntia* stems are made up of a series of joints, one growing out of another. A cactus joint is a section of stem growing out of an areole. Joints are narrow at the base, and in some species they separate easily from the plant on which they grow.

Cholla joints

Some *Opuntia* cacti, such as the very common chollas (CHOY-yuhs), have joints shaped like cylinders. Some cholla stems look like a long string of sausages. Other *Opuntia* cacti, like the eastern prickly pear shown here, have joints that are flat pads.

Opuntia leaves are usually easy to overlook. They are small, succulent, and pointed, and they grow on young cactus joints just below the areoles. They are usually one-quarter to one inch long, although they grow to two inches or more on some species. The leaves stay on the plant for only a short time. After one to three months, the *Opuntia* plant sheds them.

Ripe *Opuntia* fruits are either dry or, as on the eastern prickly pear, soft and juicy. Some *Opuntia* fruits with soft pulp are sweet and good to eat and are used as food in Mexico and other tropical countries. You can see the areoles covering the fruit. Some eastern prickly pears have spines growing in the upper areoles, others have none.

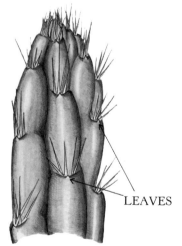

LEAVES

Leaves on a young stem in the Cactus subfamily (enlarged)

The third and last subfamily is called the Cactus subfamily. It contains all the "leafless" cacti—four-fifths of all the known cactus species. In reality, many of the plants it contains do have traces of leafy growth, but they are too small to see without a magnifier. Their leaves are just tiny lumps of tissue that appear below an areole on the growing tip of a stem. They usually disappear very soon, as the stem ages. Plants in this subfamily have no glochids. Their seeds are brown or black, without the hard white covering found in the Opuntia subfamily.

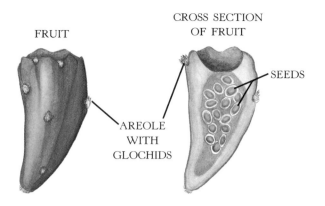

FRUIT

CROSS SECTION
OF FRUIT

SEEDS

AREOLE
WITH
GLOCHIDS

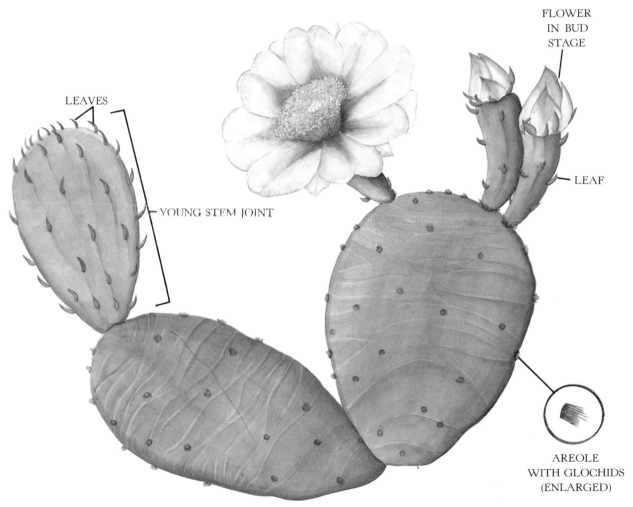

FLOWER
IN BUD
STAGE

LEAVES

LEAF

YOUNG STEM JOINT

AREOLE
WITH GLOCHIDS
(ENLARGED)

EASTERN PRICKLY PEAR CACTUS

This third subfamily includes at least thirteen hundred species distributed among eighty or more genera. It contains plants of all sizes and shapes. The smallest is the size of a button, and the largest is fifty feet tall or more, with a trunk three feet thick. All of the plants shown in the later chapters belong to this huge subfamily.

Botanists have struggled to put the vast number of plants in this subfamily into some logical order. The goal is to organize them in a way that shows how they are related to one another. Over the years, different arrangements have been suggested, but there is no final agreement on this so far.

Experts do agree that the entire cactus family needs more study before it can be understood. It is one of the largest plant families in the Western Hemisphere, and its members grow over a vast area stretching from northern British Columbia and Alberta in Canada to Patagonia at the southern tip of South America. Because there are so many species and they are so widely scattered, field research is expensive, difficult, and time-consuming.

Botanists also need good collections of preserved plant material for their research. Most plants can be preserved for study simply by drying them. But a living succulent plant, consisting mainly of water, is greatly changed when the moisture is removed. The poor quality of cactus collections has been an additional barrier to study. A distinguished botanist who has spent fifty years of his life studying the cacti thinks that the necessary research will take another century.

THREE

HOW THE CACTUS PLANT WORKS

Cactus stems are storage tanks, built to hold large amounts of water. But without some efficient system of collection, the tanks would never be filled. And without some means of conserving the store of water, they might be empty before the next rainfall.

COLLECTING WATER

Some desert plants send down long roots to tap moisture deep in the ground. Most cacti use a different strategy: they spread a wide, shallow network of roots in all directions and gather water from a large area. Even a small cactus may send its roots a distance of thirty or forty feet from the spot where it grows. One scientist who studied the root systems of desert plants said that if the desert were turned upside down, it would look like a jungle.

When the earth is dry, cactus roots are covered by a thin brown bark that seals the water inside and prevents the roots from losing moisture into the dry soil. Usually the main root system lies within the top few inches of the earth, so even a light rainfall can soak down far enough to reach the shallow network. As the rain wets the soil, small white "rain roots" grow out from the permanent cactus roots and begin to absorb rainwater. These rain roots shrivel and drop off when the ground dries, leaving only the bark-covered roots still attached to the plant.

Shallow cactus root system seen from the side (top) and from above.
Only a few roots grow down into the soil.

The shallow root system is not the only kind found among cacti. A few of the giant cacti have a thick root growing straight down in addition to the shallow roots. When its stem is filled with water, a tall plant like the giant saguaro weighs many tons. The large central root may give such a heavy plant an additional anchor in the soil.

Still other cacti have only a single large taproot and no wide-spreading network of shallow roots. Like a cactus stem, this thick root also stores water for the plant.

The largest of these turnip-shaped roots weighs fifty pounds or more and belongs to a cactus called the night-blooming cereus (SIR-ee-us). This species grows in Mexico and in the southwestern deserts of the United States. It has long, thin stems that are usually less than a yard long. Often the stems sprawl on the ground, looking like a few dead sticks. But when its blossom opens—for just a single night—the flower is large and beautiful and fills the air with an intense perfume. Its smell is said to carry through the air for a quarter of a mile.

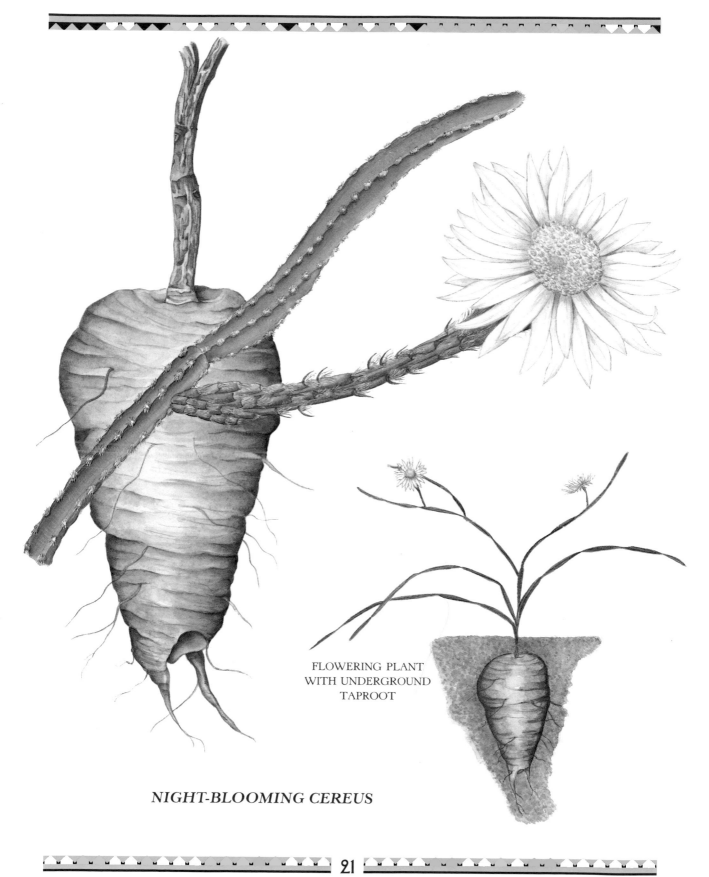

FLOWERING PLANT
WITH UNDERGROUND
TAPROOT

NIGHT-BLOOMING CEREUS

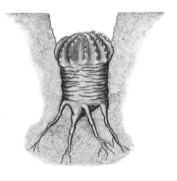

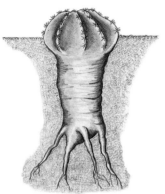

A small cactus with a large taproot, in the dry season (top) and after rainfall

Some very small cacti also have fat taproots. In addition to storing water, these roots provide the plants with another benefit. When their water content is low, taproots shrink, just as cactus stems do. As the roots shrivel, they pull the cactus stem into the ground, out of the dry air. The stems become covered by drifting soil and sometimes nearly disappear from sight. After a rainfall, the roots plump up and push the stems above ground again.

A completely different kind of root system is found among a group of plants called cactus *epiphytes*. This name comes from Greek words meaning "upon plants." These cacti grow attached to trees or rocky ledges. Most cactus epiphytes live in moist tropical forests, from Mexico down to the northern part of South America, and in the West Indies.

Cactus epiphytes may begin life rooted in the ground, but as their long, weak stems grow up into a supporting tree, the stems break and the cactus plants lose their connection to the earth. New roots sprout along the cactus stem and cling to the host. The cactus continues to make its own food, but now its water supply is limited to moisture in the air and to drops

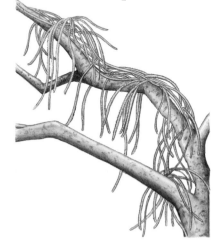

A cactus epiphyte growing on a tropical tree

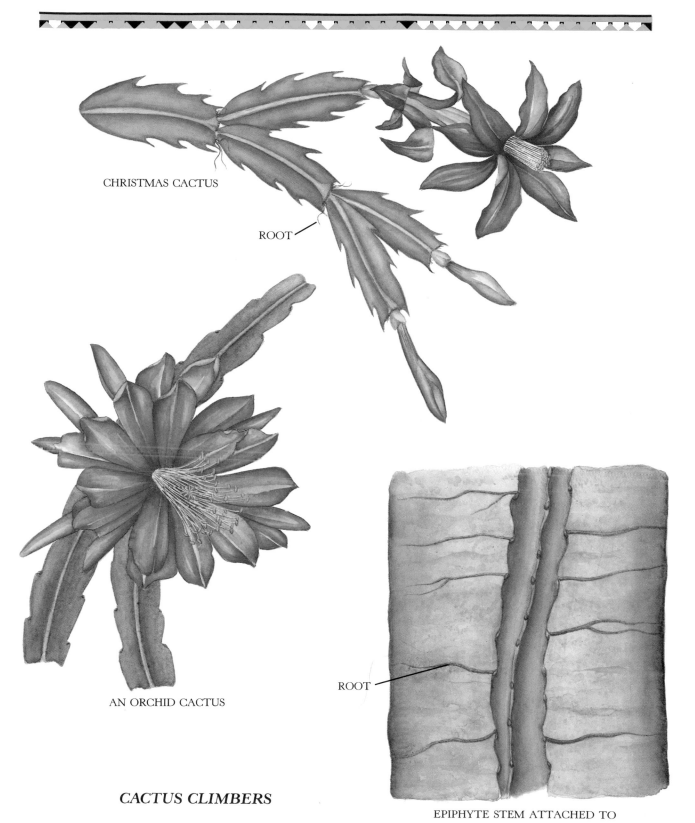

CHRISTMAS CACTUS

ROOT

AN ORCHID CACTUS

ROOT

CACTUS CLIMBERS

EPIPHYTE STEM ATTACHED TO
A TREE TRUNK

of rain that trickle down the branches of the host plant. In the thick green forests where these cacti live, very little sunlight reaches the ground. In effect, the epiphytes have traded their connection with the moist soil for a better chance to reach the sun's rays at the upper level of the forest.

Most epiphyte stems are either flat or round like thin cylinders. They have a few short spines or none at all. Christmas cactus, the common houseplant that blooms in midwinter, is a South American epiphyte. The so-called orchid cacti, popular with plant growers because of their lovely flowers, also come from the treetops.

MAKING DO WITH LESS

Water collected by root systems moves upward into plant stems and then to the growing tips of the stem, to the flowers, and to the fruits. In cactus stems, much of the water goes into storage. Cacti are misers with their water supply; they live on a daily ration that is far less than other plants need.

When you look at the stem of a desert cactus, you see that it has a shiny surface. Compared to the color of other plants, a cactus may be silvery or a dull gray-green. If you can touch its surface (without getting pricked!), it feels smooth and polished.

The shine comes from a layer of wax, a waterproof covering over the cactus skin. Just as the layer of bark seals moisture inside the cactus roots, the wax protects the stem from losing water into the air. The waxy coat dims the bright green chlorophyll under the cactus skin, giving the plant its dull color.

But the cactus could not stay alive if its green stem were completely sealed. In order to make food, plants need to take in carbon dioxide gas from the air, as well as water from the earth, and bring these materials into contact with their chlorophyll.

Plants take in the carbon dioxide through tiny pores, or openings, in their skin. And each time the pores open to allow gas to enter, some of the moisture in the stem is lost into the air outside.

Growing as a thick, leafless stem, the typical cactus has very little surface exposed to the air compared with leafy plants. And on each inch of its surface, it has fewer breathing pores. In an area that is about the size of a pinhead, most plant leaves have a hundred or more little pores. A cactus has just fifteen to seventy openings in the same amount of space on its stem.

Even more important for saving water is the timing of the food-making process in cactus plants. Cacti and other succulent plants have developed a pattern of food manufacture that is unique to them.

Chlorophyll uses the sun's energy to change raw materials into plant food. Most plants carry on the food-making process by day, opening their pores to admit air while the sun is shining. But in deserts, where so many cacti grow, high daytime temperatures with extremely dry air bring special dangers. Open pores in daylight could cause the stem to lose vast amounts of moisture into the air. The plant could easily suffer a fatal loss of water.

Most cacti avoid this danger because they make food in a two-part process. They open their pores to let in air during the night, when temperatures are cooler and water evaporation into the air is much less. The carbon dioxide from the air is changed into an acid that can be stored overnight in the cactus cells. When the sun rises, the pores close. Then, powered by the sun's rays, the chlorophyll draws upon the stored acid and goes ahead with the business of food-making.

The amount of acid in a cactus stem increases throughout the night, as long as there is room for more storage. During the day, the acid is used up. Ranch cattle that feed on cacti sometimes have indigestion after eating acid-filled plants in the early morning hours.

This unusual process of food manufacture makes it possible for cactus and other succulent plants to live in very dry climates. In the course of a summer day, for example, a column-shaped cactus standing twelve feet high loses only a little over a tablespoon of water.

While the roots and stems work to conserve the cactus's water supply, the flowers do not.

Most cactus flowers have a great many petal-like parts. Their blossoms often seem gigantic compared to the size of the plant they grow on. Some plants are almost hidden by the big flowers growing on top of their stems.

With their large, soft surface areas, cactus flowers lose a lot of water to the air and squander some of the plant's water reserves. This is the price the cactus pays for a big, showy blossom that attracts insects and other pollinating animals. The period of bloom is a short one, however, and most cactus flowers last only a day or two.

Like the night-blooming cereus, some of the largest cactus flowers blossom in the dark and avoid the drying effects of daytime heat. Many of these wilt by morning of the next day.

Night-blooming cactus flowers are white or pale yellow. Even in the dark they are visible to the moths and bats that spread their pollen, and they often have strong odors to advertise their presence.

FOUR

WHERE THE CACTUS GROWS

Cacti are native plants of the Americas. Europeans saw cactus plants for the first time after the discovery of the New World, when returning explorers brought home samples of the exotic plant and animal life of the new lands.

Since then, cacti have been planted in many parts of the world. Where conditions are favorable, they thrive. Prickly pears are now common in the countries bordering the Mediterranean Sea. In Australia, *Opuntia* cacti grew so well that they became plant pests, overrunning sixty million acres of agricultural land.

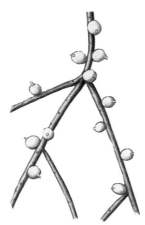

Fruit on a mistletoe cactus (This species of Rhipsalis *has spines only on young stems.)*

A few species of cacti growing in distant lands present a puzzle. The mystery plants belong to the genus *Rhipsalis* (rip-SAY-lis), which contains about fifty different species in all. *Rhipsalis* plants are called mistletoe cacti because, like mistletoe, they grow on trees and their fruit is usually a small, round berry.

Most members of *Rhipsalis* are epiphytes growing in the tropical forests of the Western Hemisphere. But a few species of mistletoe cacti have been found far from home, and no one knows how they got there. These species live in Madagascar and Sri Lanka, and on the

Areas where the "mystery" mistletoe cacti have been found in the New World (yellow) and the Old (green)

slopes of Mount Kilimanjaro in East Africa. The best guess is that the cacti were brought and planted in these distant places by people, and that birds spread the seeds into the countryside after feeding on the juicy fruits.

In the Americas, cactus plants can be found in most parts of the two continents and on their islands. In some places, they dominate the landscape. The most impressive displays—in the number and variety of cactus plants, and in the massive size of some species—grow in warm deserts that have just enough rainfall to meet the plants' water needs. In the two American continents, the centers of greatest abundance lie in areas equally distant from the equator. The North American center is from central Mexico northward to southern California, Arizona, New Mexico, and Texas.

In the United States, at least one species of cactus is native to each of the lower forty-eight states except Maine, New Hampshire, and Vermont. But the numbers fall off rapidly after leaving the warm Southwest because few species can survive freezing temperatures. Two species—one of them an *Opuntia*—reach far north into Canada. Cacti are rare east of the Mississippi. The only exception is Florida,

FRAGRANT *CEREUS*
(FLORIDA)

SILER'S BALL CACTUS
(ARIZONA)

LLOYD'S HEDGEHOG CACTUS
(TEXAS AND NEW MEXICO)

SOME ENDANGERED SPECIES

where about twelve native species grow in tropical forests along the southern coastline and in the Keys.

Although some species of cacti grow over widespread areas, most do not. A species seldom grows on both sides of a large natural barrier. For example, in South America, where the Andes mountain chain separates the west coast from the main part of the continent, the cactus populations on the two sides of the mountains are very different from each other.

Many kinds of cacti can thrive only in one particular kind of soil or climate. Some species grow only in a single valley, or on one particular mountain range. An extreme case is the little group called *Pediocactus* (ped-ee-oh-KAK-tus). Seven species have been discovered in the western United States. One is found nowhere else but on a strip of land fifteen miles long, in one particular kind of soil and rock. Because there are so few of them and because they grow only in a small area, such plants are living dangerously.

Raising cactus plants is a popular hobby. But because growing them from seeds is a slow process, the temptation to take full-grown plants from the wild is strong. Commercial suppliers sometimes meet the demand by digging up specimens from the countryside, and some amateur collectors also raid the land. Botanists writing about rare species have learned to be vague when describing their locations.

In recent years, the United States has seen large movements of population to the sun states. New commercial and housing developments in the Southwest often spill over into land that was cactus habitat. Some habitat destruction—caused by dune buggies and other off-road vehicles—is even more casual. About one-fourth of all the native cactus species in the United States are considered endangered or threatened. A few may be extinct already.

Perhaps understanding is the beginning of all caring. If that is so, the threat will matter to us only if we have some appreciation of these remarkable and unique plants.

GLOSSARY

Areole (AIR-ee-ole)—The "little area" on a cactus stem from which the spines grow.

Epiphyte (EP-uh-fite)—A plant growing on another plant or on some other kind of support, such as a rock. Unlike parasites, epiphytes growing on plants take no nourishment from the host.

Family—A plant or animal family is a group of related genera (see definition below). Families containing large numbers of genera are sometimes further divided into several

   subfamilies—Subfamilies in the same family share all the family characteristics. But each subfamily differs from the others in some significant way (or ways). A subfamily contains one or more

      genera (singular: **genus**)—A genus is a group of different kinds of plants or animals that are closely related to one another. A genus contains one or more

         species (this word is the same as a singular or as a plural noun)—A species consists of a group of plants or animals considered to be alike in all important characteristics.

Glochid (GLOH-kid)—A tiny, barbed spine, often growing in tufts, found on the areoles of cactus plants in the Opuntia subfamily.

Petaloid (PET-ahl-oyd)—The part of a cactus flower that resembles a flower petal.

Sepaloid (SEEP-ahl-oyd)—The part of a cactus flower that resembles a sepal on a typical flower.

Stem—The part of a plant that supports the leaves and flowers. The stem contains a plant's supply lines, linking these food-making and fruit-making structures to the root system.

Succulent—Juicy. In botany, a succulent is a plant with some part or parts that are thick and can store water.

INDEX

The illustrations appear in **boldface.**

Scientific names of illustrated plants

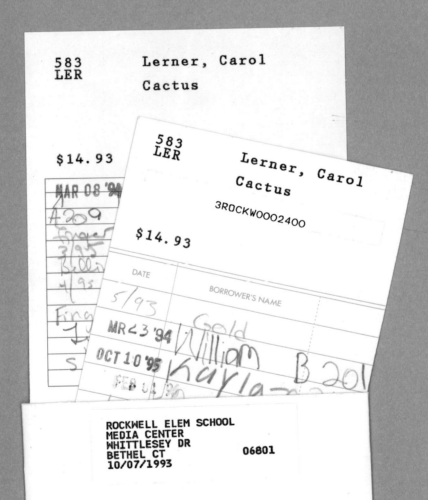

583
LER

Lerner, Carol

Cactus

$14.93

MAR 08 '94

583
LER

Lerner, Carol

Cactus

3ROCKW0002400

$14.93

DATE	BORROWER'S NAME		
5/93			
MR <3 '94	Gold William		
OCT 10 '95	Kayla	B 201	
FEB 01 96			

ROCKWELL ELEM SCHOOL
MEDIA CENTER
WHITTLESEY DR
BETHEL CT   06801
10/07/1993

BAKER & TAYLOR BOOKS